Thank you for choosing Jade Summer®.

Jade Summer® is a brand owned by Fritzen Publishing LLC, represents the work of multiple artists, and is registered in the U.S. Patent and Trademark Office.

Have a question? Please visit JadeSummer.com to learn more and send us a message.

We hope you have a great experience with this book and we appreciate your support.

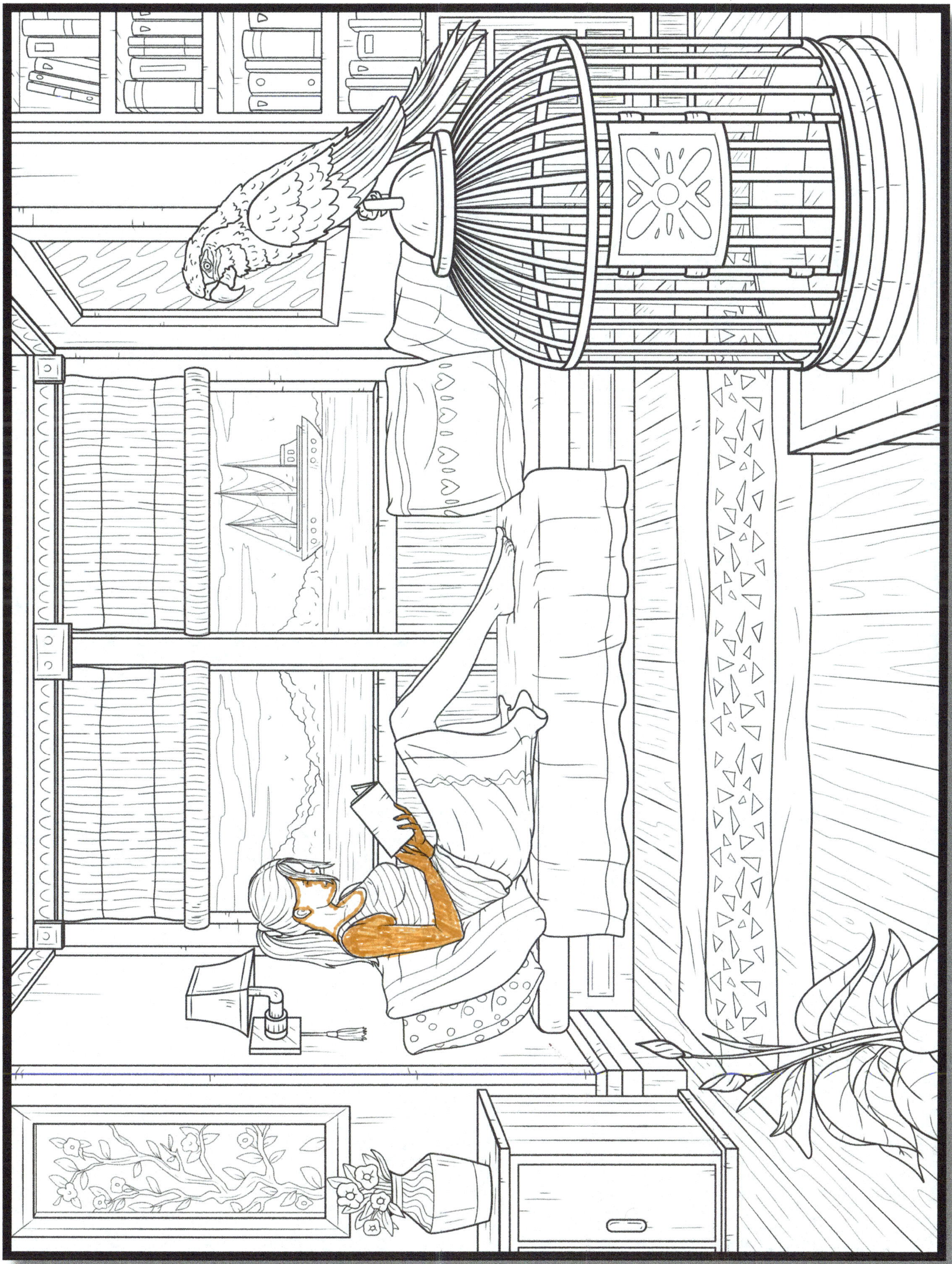

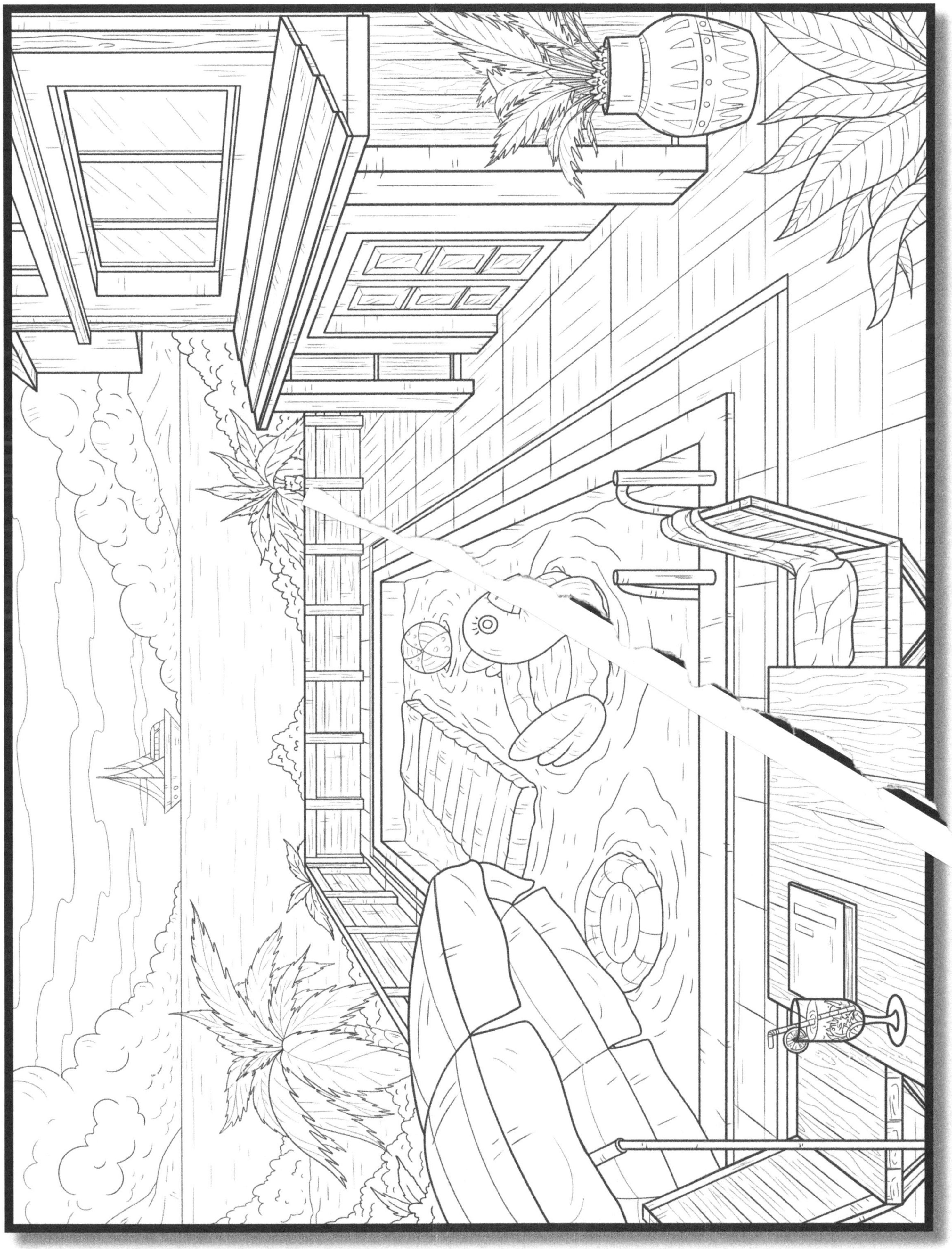

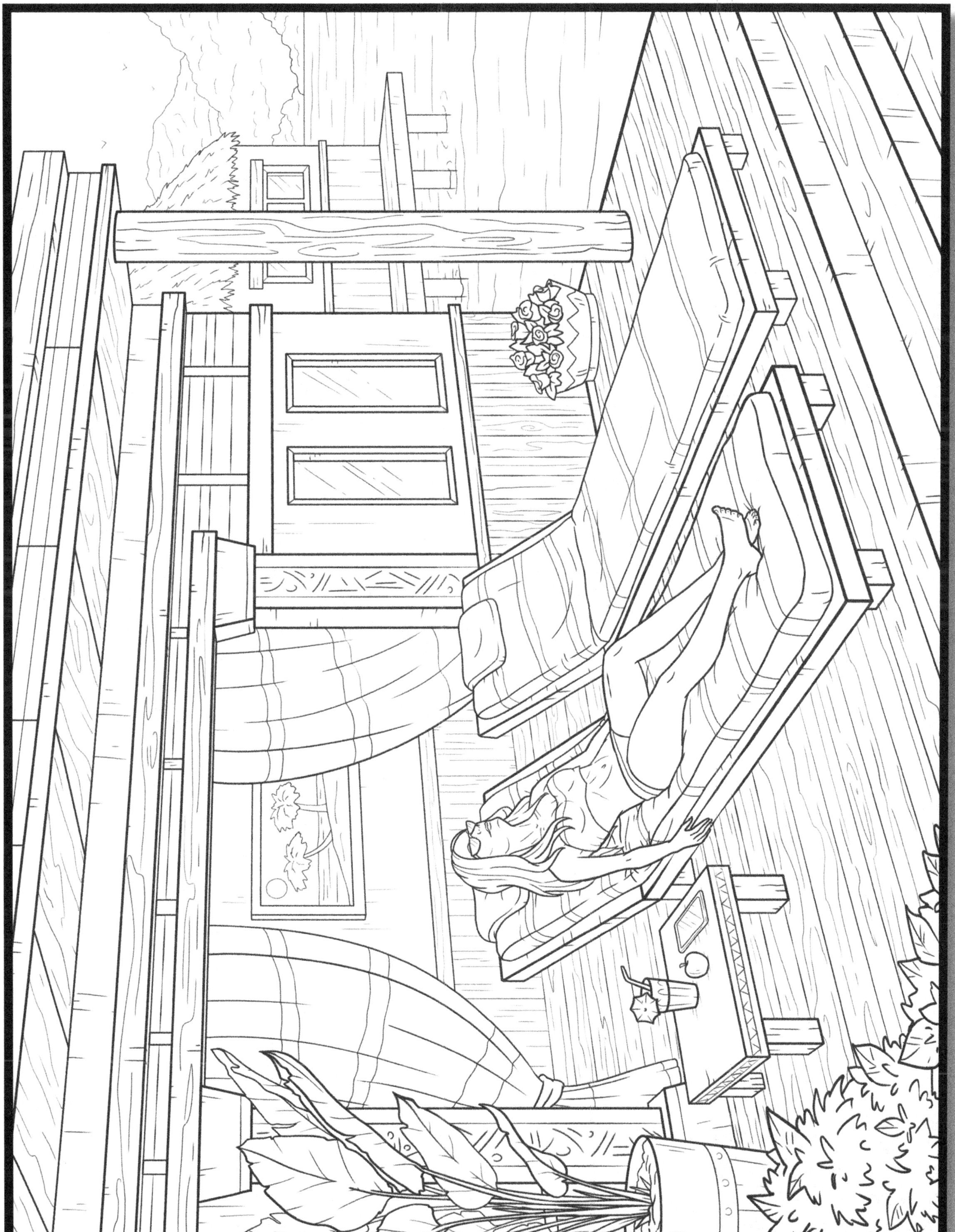

Inspirational Collection
Inspirational Quotes
Inspirational Words
Interior Designs
Intricate Flowers
Intricate Mandalas
Kawaii Fantasy
Kawaii Girls
Kawaii Grayscale
Lazy Animals
Lazy Dogs
Light Fantasy
Live Your Dreams
Love
Magical Forest
Mandalas for Beginners
Masks
Mermaids
Mermaids (2018)
Mermaids Grayscale
Mini Mandalas
Mom Coloring Book
Nightmare
Oceans
Princesses
Proud to be a Girl
Psalms
Relaxing Flowers
Secret Jungle
Sloths
Springtime Animals
Springtime Flowers
Stained Glass Flowers #1
Stained Glass Flowers #2
Stuffed Animals
Sugar Skulls
Summer
Swirls for Beginners
Tattoos #1
Tattoos #2
Tattoos Grayscale
Unicorns #1
Unicorns #2
Unicorns Grayscale
Wonderful Christmas

BONUS PAGE
COUNTRY CABINS

Made in the USA
Coppell, TX
28 July 2021

59639361R00059